Quick Tips

for Piano Teachers

A Practical Handbook for Teaching Musicianship
and Musical Independence

HILDA RY

Northwood Press

ISBN# 978-0-578-66284-8

Published by Northwood Press

Printed in the United States of America

Dedicated to

Dr. Charles Fugo
and
the memory of Dr. Max Camp

whose exceptional teaching equipped me
with principles that have served me well since 1980

and

to all my students
who have inspired fresh and creative ways
of expressing concepts.

Preface

Two extraordinary professors with whom I studied
in the late 1970s equipped me with the underlying pedagogical
principles and sequencing I use in my teaching to this day.
I am ever grateful to Dr. Max Camp, Professor of Piano Pedagogy
and Dr. Charles Fugo, Professor of Piano
at the University of South Carolina.

This book began as an outgrowth of my requirement that
students keep a permanent list of principles taught during
lessons, a practice I began for myself during my university
studies. As my students inspired me to create fresh ways
of explaining concepts, the book expanded, evolving into
what is now this resource for piano teachers.

My hope is that teachers will find this handbook a valuable
quick reference guide and keep it at their teaching piano.

Tips overlap intentionally in handbook style to provide a
more complete understanding of each topic.

– Hilda Ryan

TABLE OF CONTENTS

ALWAYS REMEMBER...

For You

Never tell a student something you can lead
them to discover by asking a question!

You get excellence when
You won't settle for anything less!

You get what you inspect
Not what you expect!

Spend most of your time
teaching what is most important to you.

"Music washes away from the soul
the dust of everyday life."
-Berthold Auerbach

"A painter paints pictures on canvas.
But musicians paint their pictures on silence."
-Leopold Stokowski

"Music is the wine that fills the cup of silence."
-Robert Fripp

"Music is liquid architecture;
Architecture is frozen music."
-Johann Wolfgang von Goethe

For Your Students

Teachers open the door.
You must enter by yourself.

You may be disappointed if you fail,
but you are doomed if you don't try.
-Beverly Sills

Dreams come true
for those who work while they dream.

Your "I will" is more important than your "I.Q."

You will never build success on what you intend to do.
Unless you put your intentions into action, nothing changes.
The only thing that ever sat its way to success was a hen!

You will never find time for anything.
If you want time, you must make it.
-Charles Buxton

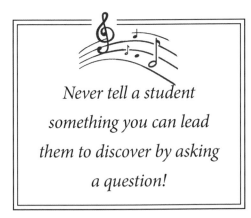

Never tell a student
something you can lead
them to discover by asking
a question!

ARTICULATION

Slurs

- <u>Release</u> at the end of all slurs and phrases rather than lifting the wrist. This prevents an accent on the following note.

- If there is a staccato on the last note of a slur, ignore it! This is over editing and the student usually ends up with an accent at the end of the slur. On the music, connect the staccato to the end of the slur.

- Avoid the tendency to push off on the second note of a two-note slur as this will make the second note louder rather than softer. Again, just release.

Staccatos

- There are at least 3 kinds of staccatos:

    - Very short   "popcorn"

    - Medium   "default"

    - Almost legato   "sticky staccato"

- Determine which staccato is appropriate based on the tempo, character and style of the piece.

    - Example: Very short staccatos are appropriate in energetic pieces, but impractical if the notes are too fast.

    - Try all three kinds of staccato and together decide which one works best. This way you develop an independent musician.

- <u>Release</u> staccatos rather than lifting the wrist.

- This prevents an accent on the following note. If the wrist lifts following a staccato, then it will drop down for the following note causing an accent. All down movements with the wrist produce a louder tone because of the faster speed of attack.

- Students have a tendency to lift and drop with both staccatos and slur breaks. Teach them to release rather than lift on both.

> **Use medium staccato as the "default" staccato.**

Portato. What's the marking?

While teaching a Bartok piece, I realized we have no mark for portato!

After puzzling over the articulation marked in the piece and beginning to look at other pieces where portato seemed to be indicated, I concluded the following.

- Since there is no "portato" articulative mark, composers and arrangers tend to use the following combinations to indicate portato:

  - Staccato notes with a slur over them

  - Tenuto notes with a slur over them

  - Staccato notes with a tenuto over them

Parallel and contrasting articulation

If contrasting articulation is not addressed in a way that allows the student to master it with ease, a reading gap often begins because the teacher is hard pressed to correct notes, fingering, dynamics as well as contrasting articulation and may resort to imitative teaching, "Here's how it goes, dear."

Teaching the basic concepts of notes, fingering and dynamics prior to introducing contrasting articulation will allow the student to focus on just this challenging reading hurdle.

- Here is one way to sequence articulative challenges.

1. **Counterpoint**—find simple original pieces with no articulation and focus on the counterpoint. Or just ignore the articulation if there is a little.

2. **Parallel articulation**—find pieces that require the same articulation in both hands. Pieces with a few measures of contrasting articulation can be rewritten or the articulation just ignored.

3. **Contrasting articulation**—find pieces with only a few measures of contrasting articulation, then move on to predominately contrasting articulation.

- Work in several books as needed to teach to these concepts. Rarely does a printed book offer this much needed sequence.

- ***Teaching Articulation: Classical Collection for Piano,*** my own published collection arranged with this sequencing, has served me well for years. (Available on Amazon.com.)

"Both-and" – both articulation and musicality

- In highly articulate styles such as the Baroque and Classical styles it is easy for students to either

    1. Observe the articulation but lose the musicality or

    2. Play musically and ignore the articulation.

- We must insist on both. In my studio I have students play with rhythmic pulse accents on the downbeat and observe the articulation before adding the phrasing, dynamics and ritards. If there is a problem, I remind them the goal is "both-and." We need both the articulation and the phrasing, etc.

Baroque articulation

- See *Style Considerations: Baroque articulation guidelines* and *More articulation consideration,* p56-57.

BALANCE

Balance is first and foremost an "ear" issue.

That is, the student must learn to hear the desired sound not only in his head, but also be able to accurately get that same sound from the piano.

Although introducing a new piece by playing it for the student will hamper their ability to sight read, demonstrating <u>musical concepts</u> like balance is essential and does not foster imitative teaching if done after the student masters the notes and rhythm.

Ask Questions

Try to avoid <u>telling</u> the student exactly what is wrong with the balance and how to solve it.

- Ask questions that will lead the student to listen more carefully. Once the student hears the problem, it is half solved!

  - Were you happy with the balance?

  - What could you do to improve it?

    - More melody?

    - Less accompaniment?

    - A combination of both?

  - Was it different this time after you made the change?

- If students are trained to listen to themselves, they can play musically anywhere, anytime on any piano. This is particularly helpful for recitals and competitions.

Two dynamic levels apart

There should be <u>two</u> dynamic levels difference between the melody and accompaniment.

- For example, if the melody is at the mezzo piano level, then the accompaniment must be played not at the piano but the pianissimo level.

- This much difference is necessary to produce excellent balance, and is characteristic of the playing of the great artists.

- Which hand takes the marked dynamic level? It varies. Sometimes it is necessary for the melody to be one dynamic level louder than marked and the accompaniment one level less. Occasionally it works best to play the accompaniment at the marked dynamic level and the melody two levels more than marked. It depends on the character of the piece and the accompaniment pattern.

- Two dynamic levels difference is particularly helpful in very quiet passages. Although the melody will likely be at a level louder than marked, the result can be strikingly effective.

Balance is always more difficult when

Keep the accompaniment "bland and boring!"

- Both hands are above middle C
- The accompaniment has faster notes, as in Alberti bass
    - There is less time for sound decay before the next note
- The hands are close together
- The melody is not on the top

Shape the phrases

- Shape the phrases with only the melody hand to avoid balance problems, particularly if the accompaniment is florid. (See *Phrasing,* p31.)

- Keep the accompaniment "bland and boring!"

Voicing

- Voicing the top note out of a chord can be difficult. Try shifting the balance of the hand toward the end of the hand with the melody note.

- Example: RH chord with melody on top—shift the balance of the hand toward the 5th finger.

"Cruise control" banned!

- Students must avoid the temptation to listen for good balance at the beginning and then forget to <u>keep listening</u>. That would be like putting your mind on "cruise control!"

  - Keep listening….and listening….and listening.

Figuration changes

Figuration changes usually bring with them new pedagogical challenges on many levels.

  - When introducing balance as a new concept, use a piece that has the same basic figuration throughout.

Balance in contrapuntal music

- Bringing out different voices in imitative music is as important to pianists as painting in a 2-dimensional or 3-dimensional style is to most visual artists.

  > **Listening to contrapuntal music with no differentiation of the voices is like looking at a painting with only one dimension.**

- We must use dynamic means to delineate the different "layers" for the listener.

  - Have the student play through the piece one voice at a time.

- Some visual students may like making a copy of the piece, highlighting each voice or fugue subject and countersubject in a different color.

- Decide which voice is most prominent in each passage or note the passages where the voices are of equal importance.

BODY-MIND COORDINATION

Moving to the meter

The body must move with the musical intent of the performer. If the practice goal is to feel the rhythmic grouping at the measure level, then the body must move with the measure if it moves and not at the beat level. If the intent is to feel the phrases, then the body must move with the phrase and not the measure.

- Allowing movement at a lower level will prevent the student from truly feeling the music at the level assigned. As a teacher, we need to watch their torso and head as well as the hands to ensure their movement matches the musical goal.

- Students should be allowed their own body movement as long as it reflects the musical intent. If it does not, then suggest perhaps a nod of the head on beat 1 for measure grouping or a movement at the phrase climax for phrasing.

- Make the body an ally. If the body can interfere with the musical goals, it can also be harnessed to help!

Musical accents

- Musical accents occur on weak beats and should not involve the body.

- The body must move with the <u>meter</u>, not with the musical accents which would reset the recurring rhythmic grouping.

  - Example: If there is a musical accent on 3 in 3/4 time, the head should move with beat 1, not beat 3.

Make your body your ally!

- Example: If a student is having a problem with syncopation, hemiola, or even note reading in a particularly difficult passage, get the body moving with the beginning of each pulse unit with perhaps a nod of the head.

- As a teacher, you can both see and hear this. If the student plays a piece with musical accents, watch their body at that point for an indication of what they are feeling inside. <u>Moving</u> with the <u>metrical</u> accents but <u>playing</u> a <u>musical</u> accent can be done and is musically rewarding!

- If the student continues to move with the musical accents, have them "ta" the rhythm with you, moving the body with the metrical accents. Then ask the student to play, keeping the same body movement with the meter. It also helps if the teacher moves with the meter while the student plays, as the student sees this in their peripheral vision. In this way, the body can be set to reflect the musical goal.

> **The body must move with the meter, not the musical accents.**

FINGERING

Changing the fingering

Before changing the fingering, try it at the performance tempo.

- Some fingerings work at a slower tempo
  but do not work at performance speed.

If the student prefers a different fingering, be sure to mark the changes in the music.

- Incorrect fingering on the music confuses the brain, takes a split second of brain processing time and often results in mistakes.

Long and short fingers

Keep the thumb on <u>white</u> notes as much as possible.

- Ideally, the long fingers 2, 3, and 4 would play on the black notes and the shorter thumb and 5th would play on the white notes.

- Of course this is not always practical, but try to avoid placing the thumb on a black note wherever possible.

  - When placing the thumb on a black note <u>is</u> necessary, the hand will need to move up <u>into the keys</u> until the thumb reaches the black notes to avoid in and out movement.

- Keep the fifth finger curved. When the weak fifth finger is allowed to play on its side, the wrist drops causing an accent.

Executing a beautiful legato

Do everything possible to use consecutive fingers on the melody to facilitate a beautiful legato.

- When a hand shift becomes necessary, try to plan the shift at a point where articulation is necessary, i.e., at the end of a slur or staccato.
- When this is not possible and an unconnected leap is necessary, use the pedal to cover the leap.

Waltz accompaniment

- This is the best way to finger a Chopin Waltz type of accompaniment:

  - Beat 1   bass note   LH finger 5
  - Beats 2-3   chords   LH fingers 1 2 4

- Accuracy is higher if the bottom note is played with finger 5 and the chord with 4 because it shortens the leap.

Hand shifts

When possible make a hand position shift coincide with an articulative release.

- Make the hand position shift a <u>horizontal</u> motion rather than lifting and putting down again which will invariably create an unwanted accent.
- Teachers who circle the finger numbers of a <u>hand shift</u> when assigning a new piece will find the student's practice more accurate. This is particularly helpful at the early elementary level.

> **Teach your students to do the "Crab Walk" instead of the "Bunny Hop."**
> (See *Technical Concepts, Moving up and down*, p60.)

HAND COORDINATION

"Doggie Paddle" not allowed!

- All experienced teachers have seen the "Doggie Paddle" in which students alternate lowering first one wrist and then the other up and down, up and down like the "Doggie Paddle." This creates musical havoc because every down wrist motion causes an accent!

- Keep the wrists still without locking them.

Hands must work as one unit

- The hands need to work as <u>one unit</u> rather than going up and down independently. Many have found that having the student lower both wrists at the downbeat and raise them slowly throughout the measure solves the "Doggie Paddle" problem. After a week of this, they should be able to eliminate this practice technique and keep their wrists still.

    - The "down and up" method may need the teacher's help initially. Demonstrate, then ask them to play while holding their wrists as they go down and up for the first few measures.

        - When the wrists come down, the heel of the hand should be on the level of the top of the keys and when they are fully raised, perhaps two inches above the keys.

    - "Down and up" involves one down movement per measure, yes, but the slow upward movement of the wrist ensures there is <u>only</u> one down motion.

MUSICAL CONCEPTS

Teaching principles

New transfer students

When I start a new transfer student, I begin by teaching concept A. When I move to concept B, I expect the student to incorporate concept A into their practice. The specific goal of concept A is in the assignment book but I do not spend lesson time explaining it again.

When I move to concept C, I expect their playing to be reflective of concepts A and B. This, coupled with having them work at their reading level, enables me to cover a lot of repertoire with them.

Concepts referred to above might range from staccatos, slurs, and two-note phrases to hand coordination, balance and the style considerations of pedal, articulation, ritard, etc.

Any new principles taught in the lesson are written in the assignment book by me and transferred at home by the student to a Principles Page in their notebook. I ask them to reread all the previous principles when they add a new one, creating an easy way to reinforce each one.

Toward musical independence

Teaching principles produces a student who is musically independent. Intermediate level students who have studied with me several years often come to the lesson after two weeks' practice with excellent balance, beautifully shaped phrases and an underlying rhythmic grouping. This allows me to spend the lesson time focusing on style considerations and the finer points of polishing.

Teaching principles fosters the kind of learning that will serve the student well past their years of piano lessons. When they pick up new music at age 35 or 55 or 75, they will still have these principles to help them understand the music from a style and theoretical point of view, as well as ways to diagnose technical problems which always cause musical problems.

The sequence of teaching rhythm, balance and phrasing

A housing contractor once built a solid foundation for a house and began to go up with the walls. He noticed that one corner of the foundation was sinking. What would you think if he ignored the problem?

We cannot afford to ignore a pulse problem any more than a contractor can afford to ignore a sinking foundation. A strong sense of rhythm is the foundation for excellent playing and must be in place before addressing balance and phrasing.

- **Rhythm:** The piece must be in "pulse" or rhythmically sound before phrase shaping can be addressed. A piece will not be beautiful if there is no underlying rhythmic reference point or pulse.

    - A teacher demonstration is very helpful here—play a phrase with a beautiful arch but pound out every beat along the way. Then ask the student if that was beautiful playing!

    - The exaggerated pulse accents used to help the student feel the rhythmic groupings at the outset of learning must be internalized at the point of adding balance and shape. (See *Rhythm: Rhythmic grouping,* p44.)

- **Balance:** The melody and accompaniment must likewise be balanced or there is nothing to shape!

    - If the accompaniment overshadows the melody, then the listener will be frustrated.

- **Phrasing:** Teach the student to arch the phrase when the rhythm and balance are in place.

    - Ensure the student is still listening for balance and underlying rhythmic grouping.

    - (See more under *Phrasing,* p32-33.)

Demonstrate <u>musical</u> concepts

- Musical concepts such as balance, phrasing, articulation, etc. are best taught with some demonstration by the teacher.

- Rhythmic reading problems, on the other hand, need to be dealt with by clapping, tapping or vocalizing the rhythm. Demonstration here does not serve the long term reading goal. (See *Rhythm: Note values,* p43.)

- Lead them to discover the rhythm by asking questions or clapping. Demonstrate musical concepts.

Communicate the form

The form of a piece needs to be made clear to the listener by the use of dynamics, articulation and time.

- **Dynamics**

  - When teaching a longer intermediate/advanced piece, each phrase has a climax, each section has a focal phrase which is most intense and the piece has a climactic point.

  - Plan louder dynamics at more important points to communicate the form. (See *Phrasing,* p31-32.)

- **Articulation**

  - When we become more intense or angry in our speaking we separate our words and emphasize each syllable to make our point. "Will-you-stop-that?"

  - As pianists, when we arrive at a big climax, making that area more articulate helps the listener know this is an important place.

    - For instance, at a cadential climax in a Bach piece, we might make the eighth notes portato instead of legato. Or if quarter notes are marked portato, we might shorten them a bit, putting more space between them for emphasis.

    - In a Classical or Romantic piece, we might separate the melody a bit for a beat or two.

- **Time**

  - The old adage "time will tell" holds true even in music if it is intelligently prepared. Those listening to an advanced student should be able to differentiate between the end of a phrase, the end of a section, and the climax of the piece by listening to the amount of ritard.

  - Save the loudest dynamic and biggest ritard for the most important place in the piece.

    > **Gauge dynamics, articulation and time liberties so they accurately convey the relative importance of those measures in the piece.**

Ritards

- Students have a tendency to use ritards as their <u>first</u> means of expression.

- When ritards or rubato are used frequently, and in the same manner, the listener is unclear which parts of the piece are most important.

  - When the big climax arrives, the listener passes it off as "just another moment" like the little boy who cried "wolf" too many times.

- Use dynamic and articulative means first, saving ritard as the <u>last</u> means of communicating form.

Gauging ritards

- Use more ritard on the <u>more</u> important points.

- Use the most ritard on the <u>most</u> important moment, keeping in mind, of course, the stylistic allowances for each period. (See *Style Considerations: General style parameters,* p56.)

  > **Too much ritard in too short a time period sounds to the listener what slamming on the emergency brakes feels like to the passenger in a car!**

- If the student has trouble feeling a gradual ritard, try movement.

  - Have them vocalize the rhythm while inscribing bigger and bigger triangles (for triple meter) or squares (for duple meter) in the air.

  - Alternately, they could conduct a larger and larger pattern in the air.

The illusion of speed

Any music on any instrument will sound like it is too slow or dragging if the pulse unit is too small.

- Example: A Bach Prelude in 4/4 will sound too slow if every quarter note is accented equally.

- A "lift" on the weak beats will give the illusion of speed. (See *Rhythm: Causes and solutions for beat level playing,* p44.)

Crescendo

- Crescendo means to get louder <u>from that point,</u> whether the starting point is loud or soft.

  - Too often a student will drop down softer to start the crescendo.

- The amount of crescendo should be determined by:

  - The **placement** in the piece

    - The climax of a section needs more crescendo than the rest of the phrases.

  - The **style** of the piece

    - Dynamic ranges differ with the styles. (See *Style Considerations: General style parameters,* p56.)

  - The **length** of the piece

    - In general, a fortissimo in an early intermediate two-page piece will not be as loud as one at the climax of a Chopin Waltz or Ballade. Trust your instincts!

Learning to listen

Our goal as teachers is to 1) "program" the best musical sound in a student's ear and 2) help them listen so they get that sound from the piano.

- When there is need for correction on a musical concept, assume the student has the correct sound "programmed" in their ear and was not listening to what was coming out of the piano. Point out what you heard and ask they to play again. If they fix it, then <u>listening was the problem</u>.

- If that does not work, then the student does not have the correct sound programmed in their ear. Talk about the style, demonstrate the musical concept to "program" it in their ear, and then ask them to play again. Follow by asking if they heard a difference in their playing. If this corrects the problem, then <u>they needed "reprogramming."</u>

- If the problem is still not corrected, then demonstrate the wrong way and right way to play and ask if they can hear the difference. Then ask them to play it the wrong and right way!

Playing contrapuntal music

- Listen to both hands melodically.

  - This will be easier if the student plays each voice separately.

  - If there continues to be a problem and the piece is two-part counterpart as in the Bach Two-Part Inventions, try moving the right hand up an octave. This gives a new prominence to the left hand and the student will hear it melodically.

Tonal decay and the matching game

- Because of the percussive nature of the piano, we must compensate for the decay of a long note by matching the following note to the decay of the previous one. The key is getting the student to listen and match.

  - Longer notes will decay considerably further and require a quieter "reentry."

  - Better quality pianos and live acoustics will sustain long notes longer, making matching a bit easier.

PEDAL

Tip of the toe

Put the tip of the toe on the tip of the pedal!
(Not literally, but it communicates the idea!)

Put the tip of the toe on the tip of the pedal!

- The pianist is more likely to clear the pedal entirely, consequently there is less blurring.

- The pianist is less likely to have an abrupt "up" motion which causes pedal noise.

- This is easier on the ankle.

Release

- <u>Release</u> the pedal rather than lifting to avoid pedal noise.

    - Think "pressure-release," rather than "down-up."

- Release hands and pedal <u>together</u> at the end of a piece.

> **Good pedaling is the result of good listening.**

- Release hands and pedal more <u>slowly</u> at the end of a quiet piece to carry the character through to the end.

    - The softer the ending of the piece, the slower the release needs to be.

    - Finishing a piece out of character, particularly releasing too quickly at the end of a soft piece, is like going to the theater and seeing the actress who plays the role of a crippled old lady straighten herself up and walk rapidly off stage in view of the audience, rather than staying in character. It ruins it!

Kinds of pedal

- Delayed Pedal — change the pedal slightly after the hand shifts
- Rhythmic Pedal — on strong beat to strengthen rhythm
- Flutter Pedal — depress completely and release a bit repeatedly
- Partial Pedal — depress 1/4, 1/2, or 3/4

Purposes for pedal

- Purposes for the piano pedal include:
  - Adding sonority
  - Blending the sounds together
  - Connecting leaps
  - Assisting the rhythm as in a touch of pedal on the downbeat of a 3/4 dance
  - Creating an ethereal sound as in Impressionistic music

> **Students must know <u>why</u> they are using the pedal in every measure and what kind of pedal.**

How much pedal?

- "Flooring it" – not in piano either!
  - Advancing students need to be comfortable with partial pedaling:

| 1/4 pedal | 1/2 pedal | 3/4 pedal | Full pedal |

- When driving a car, we decide what speed is needed and push the accelerator accordingly. We need to do the same with music. Experiment with 1/4 pedal and 1/2 pedal particularly in the Baroque and Classical styles when the use of pedal is to be used without the listener knowing it.

- How much pedal in each style?

  - *Baroque style:*   I use a little pedal and…"I know it."

  - *Classical style:*   I use some pedal and… "I know it and you know it."

  - *Romantic style:*   I use pedal generously and…
    "I know it, you know it, and I know you know it!"

  > **Pianists do not need to depress the pedal fully every time any more than a driver expects to "floor" the accelerator every time they start down the road!**

Blurred pedaling

- The pedal needs to be changed or cleared more frequently in the lower register than in the higher register because it blurs sooner.

  - Example: When playing a passage that begins with both hands low and moves up, the pedal will need to be changed frequently at first and less so as it moves higher.

- Train students to know what sound they need for the style of the piece and listen to their playing. Pianos are different. Room acoustics are different. A live room and/or bright piano will need more frequent pedal changes.

PERFORMANCES

One mistake does not a failure make!

If the listener wants perfection, it is easy enough to listen to a CD. Live performances almost always contain mistakes. Some performers just cover their mistakes better than others!

- Teach students to cover their mistakes well!

    - No "faces"

    - No stopping

    - No groaning!

- We do not want to encourage sloppy playing, but usually the student is fearful that one mistake will ruin a piece, and this is certainly not the case.

- We need to point them toward the goal of giving enjoyment to the listener and that is not dependent on a note-perfect performance. This should help the students relax and do their best.

Hearing is the key

- The student must have a definite idea of the way they want the piece to sound.

    - This is where listening to concerts and recordings is so helpful. I require students to listen to classical music one-two hours a week and attend two-three concerts per semester.

    - Listening to strong performances "programs" good sounds in a student's ear.

One mistake does not a failure make!

- Students must learn to listen differently so they hear the sound they are getting from the piano.

Performing on a different piano

When we drive a different car or ride a different bike, although the wheel or handlebars may be stiffer or the gas pedal looser, we do not insist on steering or driving it the same way as the vehicle we are used to driving. We might veer off the road! Our goal is to stay in the middle of the lane and we make any adjustments needed to accomplish that.

- When we play a different piano, we must keep the <u>sound goal</u> in our ear and <u>adjust the playing</u> so we get that sound from the piano. This is particularly helpful when students must adjust quickly to a new piano for competitions and recitals.

  - The sound should remain the same.

  - What changes is the touch and pedaling required to get that sound.

    > **Playing a different piano is a little bit like driving a different car or riding a different bike.**

Practicing for a recital or competition

- Developing mental stamina

  - Mental stamina, the ability to stay focused over a long period of time, does not just happen. It must be developed intentionally.

  - When the student can concentrate and play each piece with excellence, ask them to play two or three pieces one after the other as they would in a recital. When this is accomplished, move to perhaps a thirty-minute section of the recital, then move to the entire recital.

    - This should be done both at the lesson and at home.

Prepare with your head, play with your heart <u>and</u> your head.

- Never underestimate the mental perseverance required to play a program well to the end.

    - Remind students that athletes train to be a "4th quarter football team" or to have energy to keep running and thinking in an overtime soccer game.

    - Overtime games are often won by the team with the physical <u>and</u> mental energy to carry through to the end. We must train our students to have the same kind of mental stamina which will see them through to the finish.

- Review early practice methods up to and especially the day of the performance. This will prevent the performer from losing sight of the foundational concepts in their playing.

- Practice the response to a memory lapse. Plan "jump ahead" spots. Then, at the lesson, stop the student and ask them to jump ahead to the next starting spot. Never allow them to go back as they might make the same mistake.

Recital order

- **For the performer's sake,** choose an easy piece to begin the program to allow nerves to settle, because pieces with lots of 16th notes will be uneven if the performer is nervous.

- **For the listener's sake,** plan the heavier pieces toward the beginning when the listeners' concentration is at its best.

Memory strength

Teach students to cultivate analytical and aural memory as well as the visual and kinesthetic.

- Memory based on all of these methods is immeasurably stronger than only the visual or only the aural, much as a 3-strand rope is stronger than a single-ply one.

- The aural and particularly the analytical memory are best taught by the teacher at the lesson.

Oxygen for the brain

The physical matters too!

- To reach our performance potential, we must ensure the brain has adequate oxygen.

    - Breathing: Teach students to take a few deep breaths prior to performing. This provides oxygen to the brain and has a calming effect on the body.

    - Blood flow: Tension in the shoulders will restrict blood flow and oxygen to the brain. Teach students to shrug their shoulders a few times before a performance.

- Sip water prior to playing or during breaks in a recital.

- It is helpful to breathe through a difficult passage.

    - When approaching a difficult passage, take a deep breath. Sometimes we hold our breath without realizing it and cut off the necessary oxygen.

    - Write "breathe" in the music as a reminder for practice and performance. I find this extremely helpful myself.

PHRASING

A phrase is a "musical sentence"

- Other comparisons to reading include:
    - A phrase is like a sentence.
    - A section is like a paragraph or chapter.
    - A piece is like a chapter or book.

Characteristics of Phrasing

- Phrases are at least four measures long.
    - Two-measure groupings are sub-phrases.
    - Four-measure phrases are common in the Classical style.
        - When asking a student to mark the ends of phrases for the first time, try to choose a piece with predictable with four-measure phrases like the Classical style if students are reading literature.
- Phrases have three parts—
    1. Ascent to climax,
    2. Arrival at climax, and
    3. Descent.
        - Listen for effectiveness in all three areas of the phrase.
        - Drawing a curve in the air depicting the phrase slope is an effective visualization.

Phrase climaxes

- Phrases have one climax point, usually in the last half of the phrase. Bartok is a notable exception, with accents often at the end the phrase in the middle of the measure.

- Phrase climaxes are determined by one or more of the following factors:

  - Melodic high point

  - Rhythmic change

    - Isolated slow note in fast passage

    - Faster notes in slower passage

  - Harmonic interest

    - A point of dissonance

    - A point of surprise harmony

    - A harmonic destination point

- Examples are pointed out in **Teaching Articulation: Classical Collection for Piano,** p8. (Available on Amazon.com.)

Every measure has a musical "I.D."

Shaping the phrases

- Have the student exaggerate the phrase shape at first and smooth it out later if it is too much.

- Shape the melody only.

  - Keep the accompaniment "flat" or "bland and boring!"

- Listen for each part of the beautifully arched phrase.

  - Sometimes the ascent begins too late and the climax is not reached.

  - Sometimes the climax sounds like an accent rather than an arrival point.

  - Sometimes the climax is not big enough.

  - Sometimes the descent drops off too suddenly rather than tapering off.

- The amount of ritard allowed at the point of climax will depend on the style. (See *Style Considerations: General style parameters*, p56.)

Teaching phrasing

- Gradually teach the student to identify the phrase ends and climaxes for themselves.

- Allow for differences of opinion as to the location of the climax, provided it can be substantiated and they can play it convincingly.

  1. At first, mark everything for the student with the goal of teaching shaping.

  2. Begin to explain the markings on the music to the student as you write them. Think out loud with the student. (See *Phrase climaxes,* p32.)

  3. Assign the student to mark the ends of the phrases at home and do the climaxes together at the next lesson.

  4. Finally, have the student mark everything and discuss it at the lesson. This is part of developing an independent musician!

- Break between phrases with a <u>release</u>, not an up motion.

- Keep phrasing difficulty in mind when choosing music.

  - The slower the tempo, the harder it is to play in pulse and to turn beautiful phrases.

    - Slow sonata movements or any slow pieces are much more difficult to play musically. Be sure the student is capable of a musical performance before choosing slower pieces for a recital.

  - The more articulation required, the harder it is to focus on beautiful phrases.

    - Classical sonatas in general, and Haydn in particular, are more difficult in this regard.

    - The Classical style is ideal for introducing phrase length and shape but has articulative challenges.

    - Baroque pieces with constant articulative demands are also more challenging.

    - Romantic style pieces are an ideal place to introduce phrase <u>shape</u> because articulation is minimal.

Phrasing in Baroque music

- Planning phrasing in Baroque music is probably the most difficult.

    - Identify the cadence points.

    - Note the sequences and episodes. In <u>imitative</u> Baroque music,

        - Sequences involve the spinning out of an idea, often using the circle of fifths.

        - Episodes involve music other than the motive or subject (or "other stuff" in kid talk).

    - Cadences are often destination/climax points in Baroque style.

    - Sequences and episodes need either a crescendo or diminuendo.

        - The melodic direction is sometimes a clue as to the direction.

        - A melodic ascent may sound natural with a crescendo, for example. But not always.

- Because it is more difficult to mark the phrases and climaxes in Baroque music, introducing phrase <u>length</u> is best done in the Classical style with their predictable four-measure phrases.

- Be sure every measure is moving toward or away from a climax. Nothing puts a listener to sleep faster than a Baroque piece with a pulse level of a quarter note and flat dynamics!

- If the phrase is too long to manage one gradual crescendo to the climax as is often the case in more difficult Baroque works, then plan a secondary climax point.

Every measure has a phrase "I.D."

- Students should always play with an awareness of where they are in the phrase.

    - Each measure is part of the ascent to the climax, arrival at the climax, or movement away from the climax of the phrase.

    - As such, every measure has a phrase "I.D."

- Stop a student's playing anywhere, and they should be able to tell you the measure's phrase "I.D."!

PRACTICING

Practice is problem solving

- I require a parent of students twelve years and younger to come to the lesson and to practice with their child at home. Students of this age cannot problem solve or stay on task for any length of time.

- I have found this true even if the child is unusually gifted. The parent makes the difference between good preparation and excellent preparation.

- If the parent has no musical background, I assure them that they can learn along with the child. It's a "two-fer" – a two-for-one!

- Because excellent progress is predicated on excellent practice, problem solving is the key to progress.

Practice is problem solving.

- This happens only if the assignment has specific goals for each piece and the student reads the specific assignment for each piece at every practice.

Perfect practice

- Practicing literature with 95% accuracy is possible when

    - Working at their reading level

    - Working on only one or maybe two goals at a time on a given piece

    - Working slowly enough to maintain 95% accuracy rate

> **Playing a passage wrong three or four times and correctly only once is like "ironing in a wrinkle."**

- If the student has multiple problems after playing the passage twice, a different game plan is needed lest the wrinkle be ironed in.

    - Try slower, simpler, or change to easier music.

- Repetitions on isolated spots must be perfect to ensure progress in the right direction!

- It is better <u>not to practice</u> than to practice wrong because incorrect practice creates sounds in the ear which will need to be reprogrammed. Repeating mistakes is like "ironing in a wrinkle.'"

Practice smart

Perfect practice makes perfect.

- Work with the student until <u>they</u> can hear their own mistake and know when they have corrected it. At that point they can go home and practice effectively.

- Make the corrections at the lessons, then ask the student to <u>tell</u> you what changes they made to correct the problem.

- When students hear their mistakes at a lesson and stop to fix it, they deserve praise, because the first step toward solving the problem is having <u>them</u> hear the problem.

Practicing before a performance

- Just before a performance, review early practice methods. This includes going back to practicing without time liberties.

    - Never returning to practice without ritards may result in the student taking more and more time liberty without realizing it, like the lady who puts on more and more perfume because she does not smell it anymore.

    - Going back to no time liberties (the equivalent of no perfume) provides a new reference point that is invaluable. Think of it as a musical "reboot!"

Practicing the first week

- <u>Do require:</u>
    - Notes and rhythm
    - Fingering
    - Pulse accents
    - Look up musical terms
- <u>Do not require:</u>
    - Musical accents
    - Pedal
    - Ornaments
    - Articulation

You should see a little bit of progress on every piece every day.

Note: Intermediate/advanced students can often handle pulse and articulation the first week.

Troublesome spots

- Stop on the wrong note!
    - If <u>only one note or chord</u> is consistently wrong, try playing a measure or two prior to that note and stopping <u>on that note or chord</u>. Somehow the brain makes the correction! It works every time!
- Isolate <u>difficult spots</u> at a slower tempo and repeat them 10X <u>perfectly</u>.
    - Sometimes the fastest way there is "slower!"
- Isolating <u>sections</u> and practicing them at different tempi is fine.
    - When practicing the entire <u>piece</u>, however, a consistent tempo must be maintained.
    - When playing the whole piece, simplify any spot that is too difficult to play at the tempo of the rest of the piece,
        - At the difficult spot, play just one hand or "ta" the rhythm.
        - Simplifying is "incomplete" playing which does not have to be "reprogrammed" in the student's ear later.

- Changing the tempo, however, is something that will require "reprogramming" and must be avoided.

- Is there a technical problem?

  - Teachers diagnose technical problems using both what they see and what they hear.

  - See *Technical Concepts: Hand movements,* p59-60.

- Would analysis help?

  - Lead the student to discover the harmonies in the passage.

  - Look for rhythmic, harmonic or melodic patterns.

> **Avoid any practice method that will require "reprogramming"**

Convincing them to isolate

There is a lot to be said for ten perfect, slow repetitions, but students groan at the idea of repeating spots ten times and sometimes need a pep-talk.

I once asked a new student who had not made progress on his goal for the week on a certain piece to tell me how he had been practicing. To my dismay, he replied, "I played up to this point (indicating the problem area) and went back to the beginning because I had made a mistake."

After picking my chin up off the floor, I took a piece of paper and drew a path through the woods with a log fallen down across the middle. I then drew a bicycle and asked him what he would do if he was riding on that path, found a log in the path and there was no way around it.

After coming up with all the possibilities he could think of, I asked what he would think of someone who rode his bike up to the log, turned around and went back to the beginning. He then started out again, got up to the log, turned around and went back, etc., etc.

He got the point without me even having to make the application to his piece!

General guidelines

- Practice fast pieces slowly…
  To conquer technical difficulties

- Practice slow pieces fast…
  To make it easier to hear the phrasing

- Practice loud pieces softly…
  To listen to the sound quality

- Practice soft pieces with more sound and relaxed arm…
  To get in the ear the resonant tone needed

Zooming in and out

- "Zooming in and out"

  - Begin the study of a piece with a "zoom out" look at the form.

  - Then "zoom in" to learn the small pulse units and phrases.

  - Finally, "zoom out" again to plan the climax of each section and finally the climax of the piece.

- This learning sequence is based on the architectonic structure of the piece.

Homophonic and contrapuntal pieces

- **Homophonic** - practice music hands together

  - No need for hands separate except for particularly difficult spots if the piece is at the student's reading level.

- **Contrapuntal** – practice one voice at a time, then various combinations

  - If the music is 2-part counterpoint, try taking the right hand up an octave.

    - This makes it easier to hear both hands independently, especially the left hand.

    - Too often students play contrapuntal music listening primarily to the right hand.

Practice assignments

- Be sure to give assignments with specific goals.

    - For example, "taper the descent of your phrase more gradually" is clearer than "more expressive" or "p. 21."

- Require students to keep the assignment book on the music rack and refer to each piece's goals during practice.

- If a student does not reach an attainable practice goal on a piece and has no viable excuse, I rewrite the same assignment in red. This draws their attention to it during practice as well as mine at the next lesson. In addition, it provides an easy way for the parent to check on the student's practice habits. No red means they are practicing smart!

> **Practice should never be <u>boring</u>.**
> **Tedious at times, yes, but never boring**
> **if the student is focusing on a specific**
> **goal with every repetition.**

Practice should never be <u>frustrating</u>

- When students practice smart with specific goals in mind, it should not be difficult for the family to hear practicing at home and should not be frustrating for the student.

- If practice is frustrating, stop and diagnose the problem.

    - Are there too many goals? Focus on one at a time.

    - Try the **SSS Solution:**

        - Slower

        - Shorter

        - Simpler

Engage your brain before engaging your fingers!

Listening and thinking are keys

- Engage your brain before engaging your fingers!

- Don't substitute a practice method, no matter how good, for <u>listening</u> to yourself.

- Save "automatic pilot" for the planes and "cruise control" for cars!

  - Emphasize to your students the importance of practicing only when they can focus and problem solve.

- If the student finds the mind slipping into "cruise control" teach them to

  - Take a drink of water

  - Practice a different piece

  - Talk to themselves about the goal and refocus their thinking

  - If all this fails, finish practicing later, even if it means the student does not get any more practicing done!

    - No practice or a shorter practice is better than incorrect practice.

    - Incorrect practice "irons in" the wrinkles and it will take twice as long to unlearn the wrong sound in the ear!

- Remind students every time they put their hands on the piano they are "programming" their ears and mind with those sounds. Teach them to get in the habit of <u>purposeful playing</u>.

- Teach them to evaluate their playing every time they stop. They need to practice until they see a little bit of progress on every piece every day.

RHYTHM

Note values

When a student has trouble getting the note values, try one of these methods.

- **Counting aloud**

  - When counting aloud, the goal is for the voice to lead the fingers. Make sure the student uses their "soccer field" voice.

    - A soft voice will follow the fingers and the student will continue to play the wrong rhythm.

    - Counting aloud only works if the voice is loud enough to direct the hands.

- **Counting off**—reading a piece the first time

A few years ago I prepared a college piano major to pass a sight-reading exam. Not only did "counting off" enable him to pass the exam, it has helped my students as well since then! It is amazing how well this works. Counting off seems to set up a rhythmic groove.

1. Count two measures aloud with the student, emphasizing the first beat. Use a sight-reading tempo. **1**-2-3

2. Count the rhythm of the first two measures aloud together saying simply "ta-ta-ta" for the rhythm of the melody, again emphasizing beat 1.

3. The student plays four measures with no one counting.

4. Stop and ask the student, "Did that rhythm match your ta-ta rhythm?"

   - If the answer is yes, then ask them to begin again and continue on.

   - If the answer is no, or should be no, then repeat #1 to #3 again.

Rhythmic grouping

Help your students feel the rhythmic grouping. One way to help feel the music's underlying rhythmic unit is to add a temporary accent (pulse accent) at the beginning of the rhythmic unit, which is most often the measure.

This practice measure "programs" the rhythmic reference point in the student's ear. When the student has internalized the rhythmic unit, the external accent can be removed, leaving the rhythmic impression which gives life to the playing.

Causes and solutions for beat level playing

If the student has been asked to put an accent on beat 1 and feel a lift for the other beats but still plays at the beat level, here are the probable causes.

- Rhythmic problem

    - Problem   Not feeling the lift on the weak beats

    - Solution   Move with them

        - Bounce a ball in the air coming up slowly

        - Sway left and right with both hands in the air

        - Use "washing windows" movement

- Technical problem

    - Problem   Dropping with the wrist

    - Solution   Keep the wrist still

- Body movement problem

    - Problem   Moving the head with the beat
                       instead of the measure or the
                       measure instead of the phrase climax

    - Solution   Suggest they nod their head with the
                       measure or phrase climax,
                       depending on the assignment

Body movement reflects musical intent

Since we diagnose as teachers with both our eyes and ears, notice their body movement. While we want to allow the student to move naturally, sometimes this can get in the way. The body can be an ally if it aids in sensing measures or phrases, but can be the enemy if the head nods or the toe taps at a level below the one in which the student is focusing.

The body must mirror the musical intent.

It is impossible to move at the quarter note level and play at the measure level. Likewise, it is impossible to move with the measure and shape a beautiful phrase. Try it! The body must mirror the musical intent.

If the student is moving too frequently for the musical goal of either pulse or phrasing, then gently suggest they shift movement to the desired level.

Engage the body as an ally. Put in motion some kind of movement, perhaps a nod of the head at the beginning of each pulse unit if the student is working on pulse, or at the climax of the phrase if the student is working on phrasing.

Musical accents

- If there are <u>musical accents on weak beats</u> the student must avoid the tendency to move with them. Rather, keep the body movements with the natural accents on the strong beats and feel the pull against it when the musical accents are played.

- Watch the student's movements when they play musical accents and suggest a movement with the <u>meter</u> if they are moving with the musical accents.

- If this does not solve the problem immediately, have the student stand and together with them make some large movement such as "washing windows" with the meter and vocalize the piece's rhythm, emphasizing the musical accent with the voice but keeping the body moving with the metrical, natural accent.

- When the body is coordinated with the meter and musical accents are felt as rhythmic dissonance, there is a wonderful sense of being inside the rhythm musically.

Ritards

- No ritards while learning notes

  - When they have mastered the rhythm and move to phrase shaping, then add the ritards.

  - Utilize a ritard only after exhausting other means such as dynamic, pedal, articulation, etc.

- Gauge the ritard to fit the position in the piece.

  - More ritard for a more important place.

  - Less ritard for a less important place.

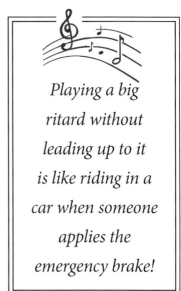

Playing a big ritard without leading up to it is like riding in a car when someone applies the emergency brake!

- If a student has trouble feeling a graduated ritard try having them conduct a pattern with you.

  - Make the pattern bigger with every measure. This makes an **automatic graduated ritard** which the student will notice with both hands and ears as well if they are counting out loud.

    - Try inscribing a four-sided box for 4/4 time for each measure.

    - Try inscribing a triangle or Christmas tree shape for 3/4 time for each measure.

  - Make the pattern get bigger with every measure, counting 1-2-3 or 1-2-3-4 aloud and you have a nicely graduated ritard every time!

The metronome—help or hindrance?

When practicing an advanced classical piece that requires beginning at a very slow tempo and gradually increasing the tempo, use the body as an ally by creating a body movement that moves with the pulse unit rather than the beat level given by the metronome.

Count in your head, not with your wrist!

- Some beginners count quarter notes with a wrist drop on each one. The same wrist movement on every quarter note gives each beat the same emphasis.

- Encourage them to keep the wrists still and count in their head.

Count in your head, not with your wrist!

Rhythm first

- Since rhythm is foundational for music that captivates the listener, we must ensure that our playing conveys rhythmic vitality before considering balance or phrasing.

- See *Musical Concepts: The sequence of teaching rhythm, balance, and phrasing,* p18.

Difficult passages

- Quite often, the student's focus shifts from measure groupings or phrasing to beats in difficult passages. Listen for this. Make certain the underlying rhythmic groupings are maintained even when the passage is difficult.

- Shifts in rhythmic grouping size are perplexing to the listener. If they have been tapping their foot to the measure, and the pianist begins to accent every beat in a difficult passage, the listener will stop tapping.

SIGHT READING

Counting off

If the student has a problem with the starting rhythm in a new piece, count off first with the student.

- Count two measures aloud together with an emphasis on beat 1.

- "Ta" or clap the rhythm of the melody's first two measures together.

- The student plays four measures with no counting and stops.

- Ask the student if the rhythm matched the "ta." If it did, then they begin again and keep going. This keeps them listening.

This works like a charm for me at any level or aged student. It's something I developed to help a college student pass his sight reading test.

If you let your fingers catch up to your eyes, you're in "deep puddin'!"

- The eyes must read ahead of the fingers much as we do when reading words.

- Quite often the problem is not reading large enough groups of notes. Reading patterns and recognizing harmonic movements facilitates this.

- See *Sight Reading: Seven sight reading secrets*, p51.

If you let your fingers catch up to your eyes, you're in deep puddin'!

Beginners: Landmarks and intervals

- Read by interval from the landmark.

    - Find the starting note by noting its position in relation to a landmark.

    - Read by interval from there.

- Reading by interval from landmarks is the equivalent of phonetic reading.

    - A person who learned to read phonetically can sound out any word using pronunciation principles.

    - A pianist who reads by intervals can read any notes using the landmarks as guideposts and move by interval from there.

- Reading by interval from landmarks is like knowing how to get to a friend's house using street landmarks.

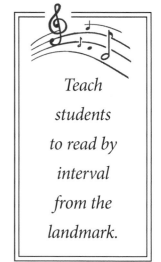

Teach students to read by interval from the landmark.

- *A Max Camp illustration:*

    If Susie moves into the neighborhood, she can either get to Cindy's house by having Cindy come over and take her there every time, or learn to get there herself by noting some landmarks such as turning left at the church, going two blocks and making a right at the red house, etc.

    Having Cindy come over to take her may work fine for finding Cindy's house, but think what it means when Susie wants to go to Alexa's house, and Jane's house and Cameron's house. She is stuck at home until someone comes to lead her there. Learning her way around using local landmarks gives her an immediate independence.

    - So, in reading music, starting with the note's relative position to a landmark and reading by interval from there frees the student to read much more quickly and fluently.

The student will learn to read this way only if the teacher addresses every wrong note with the question, "How far was this (wrong) note from the previous note?" or, "How far is this note from a landmark?" Giving the student the correct note and saying, "No, this is a G," does not further fluent reading and musical independence.

Setting your face!

- If the student is primarily reading the music

  - Have them set their face on the music and glance down at their fingers when needed without moving their head.

- If the student is playing primarily from memory

  - Have them look down at their fingers and glance up with their eyes at the music when needed without moving their head.

Seven sight reading secrets

1. Look for patterns

   - Look for rhythmic and melodic patterns

   - This, combined with reading vertically, can cut down significantly on the number of items to be "processed" and will accelerate reading.

2. Read in groups of notes

   - Much as you do when reading a book.

3. Read ahead

   - Much as you do when reading a book.

4. Hear ahead

5. Read vertically and harmonically

   - Identifying the chordal structure allows the reader to process what he sees more quickly.

   - Learning triads and inversions and learning to recognize chords is time well spent at the lesson and practicing at home.

6. Keep your eyes on the music. Feel instead of looking down, using the black notes as landmarks. (See *Sight Reading: Feel your way,* p52.)

7. Play in rhythmic groupings or pulse

   - Amazingly, playing in rhythmic groupings or pulse helps reading! The ear pulls the eye along and somehow facilitates faster reading.

Feel your way

- Feel your way around the keyboard as much as possible. Looking down slows the reading.

  - Practice octave moves of 3rd, 4ths, and 5ths looking and then not looking at the hands.

  - Organists play without looking at their feet very often because they learn the feel of certain intervals and also because they feel the black pedal notes with their toes and use them as landmarks. In the same way, pianists can learn to feel the black notes with their fingers and feel their way around.

Read the interval first, then the finger number

- Finger numbers are usually (not always) given when there is a hand position shift. If the student reads the finger number first they will probably play the wrong note.

- Teach students to read the interval first, then the finger number.

SOUND CONCEPTS

A bell-like sound

- A bell or chime-like sound is achieved with a fast attack of the fingers and a quick upward motion of the wrist to release it.

A bright or warm sound

- Playing on the tip of the fingers produces a bright and more percussive sound.

  - This is particularly desirable for Classical style pieces and percussive works like some of those by Bartok, Prokofiev, etc.

  - The sound will be brighter to almost brittle dependent on the amount of cushion on the tip of the finger, the piano, and room acoustics.

    - The less cushion on the pad of the finger, the brighter the sound.

    - The more cushion, the more mellow the sound.

- Playing on the ball or pads of the fingers produces a warm singing tone.

  - This sound is preferred particularly in the Romantic works such as those of Chopin, slow Classical sonata movements, etc.

  - Apparently Artur Rubenstin had large fingers with big pads which accounts at least in part for his warm tone. (*Basic Principles in Pianoforte Playing* by Josef Lhevinne p.14.)

A substantive sound

- A substantive but not too focused sound (as in the left hand downbeat of a waltz) is produced by:

    - Keeping close contact with the keys

    - Playing on the balls of the fingers

    - Making a fast attack

Fortissimo

- When playing fortissimo, start with a level wrist and finish with an upward movement with the hand rather than coming down into the keys from above.

    - This produces a sound that is both powerful and pleasing, unlike the sound created when the performer comes down into the keys from above.

    - If more sound is needed, play with a faster attack and engage the weight of the torso by leaning into the piano from the waist and, if necessary, come off the bench an inch or two!

STYLE CONSIDERATIONS

Integrating style into the lesson

Begin teaching style considerations with the early repertoire such as the Bach Minuets, sonatina movements and the Schumann *Album for the Young*. Require students to memorize the style period dates and composers and mention these terms and styles as you teach.

- Call for pieces at the lesson by composer names. It is worthwhile to write both the style and composer abbreviations in the assignment book.

Baro	Bach	book, p. 12	pulse & articulation
Class	Clem	book, p. 27	shape phrases
Rom	Schum	book, p. 15	dynamics
Cont	Bartok	book, p. 35	review

- Choosing literature editions

  - Before choosing literature, be sure you agree with most of the articulation on the Baroque and Classical pieces. It is time consuming and messy to redo what is printed.

  - Performance practice today calls for more detachment in the Baroque and Classical styles than it did 50 years ago.

- New transfer students

  - Because of the inherent articulative difficulties in Baroque and Classical style, it is easier to begin work with a new student using Romantic style literature where the focus can be on the musical concepts of balance and phrasing.

- Style corrections

  - When making style corrections, be sure to reference the style parameters (see *General style parameters,* p56).

For example, instead of saying, "That's too much ritard. Play it again with less," say, "That ritard is a bit outside the scope of what is acceptable in the Classical style."

- This explains why you are making the correction and helps them understand the style.

General style parameters

Mention these parameters as you teach. Comparing and contrasting is one of the best ways to learn.

	Baroque	Classical	Romantic	Cont'porary
Dynamic range	Small	Expanded	Exploits limits	Varies
Keyboard range	Limited	Expanded	Exploits limits	Varies
Keyboard texture	Thin	Thin	Thick	Varies
Ritard allowances	1-2 beats	1-2 measures	Several mm.	Varies
Pedal allowances	Very little	Some	Often full	Varies
Dissonance lasts	1-2 beats	1-2 measures	Several mm.	Varies, or not resolved
Driving force	Heart	Head	Heart	Varies
Common forms	Dances	Sonata	Descriptive	Mixture

Baroque articulation guidelines

- Connect stepwise movement.
- Detach leaps of a 4th or more (3rds depend on context).
- Connect fast notes of any interval.

More Baroque articulation considerations

- The above guidelines need to be tempered by tempo and the character of the piece.

  - Fast notes need to be connected even if they are leaps.

  - Slow notes may need a portato touch even if they are stepwise.

  - Adjust articulation to the character of the piece. The teacher makes a subjective call based on their knowledge of the styles. For example, an energetic piece with relatively fast notes may sound better if slightly detached.

- More articulation is usually needed at:

  - Cadence points

  - Climax points (which are often cadence points as well in the Baroque style)

- The more important the area, the more articulation is needed.

Ornamentation

- Baroque and Classical

  - Begin on the beat from the note above unless it cause a "stutter."

  - These add "zing" or "zest" as they accentuate the dissonance, a bit like adding cayenne pepper to a dish.

- Romantic

  - Begin before the beat on the principal note.

  - These add beauty and grace and are designed to adorn the melody.

  - Exceptions: Chopin and Schubert clung to the Baroque/Classical ornamentation rules.

    - One way of helping students remember these two composers is by saying,

      - "SsshhChopin and ssshhSchubert ssshhied away from the new ways of ornamentation."

- While Chopin and Schubert's ornaments are executed in the Baroque manner, the spirit and sound of the music is steeped in the Romantic tradition.

- Grace notes are to be executed with grace and élan, a contrast to the zing of the Baroque style even though the dissonance occurs on the beat.

- A helpful reference manual to keep at the piano is *Ornamentation, A Question and Answer Manual,* by Watts/Bigler (Alfred Publishing).

TECHNICAL CONCEPTS

View helpful videos on technique at
YouTube channel: Hilda Ryan.

Technical problems

- All technical problems cause musical problems which is why they must be diagnosed and solved.

Technical problems always cause musical problems.

Hand movements

Up and Down Movement

- Every down movement with the wrist produces an accent—wanted or not!

- Play on the tip of the 5th finger and the corner of the thumb to avoid down movements and unwanted accents.

- Avoid the temptation to raise and lower the hand at the end of every slur or staccato in highly articulated music.

  - It causes unmusical accents. Rather, keep the hand close to the keys.

In and out movement

- In and out movement of the wrist causes unevenness.
- Stay up in the keys when playing passages with black notes to prevent unnecessary movement.

Moving up and down the keyboard (left and right)

- When shifting hand positions, avoid lifting the wrist as that will require dropping back into the keys resulting in an accent. Rather, make a smooth <u>horizontal</u> movement hugging the keys as much as possible.

- Teach students to do the "Crab Walk" not the "Bunny Hop" when making big leaps.

  - **"Bunny Hop"**

    - Movement up in the air and down again to a new note creating an unwanted accent, like rabbits whose movement is usually a hop.

  - **"Crab Walk"**

    - The sideways movement to another note that avoids a drop into the key with an accent, like crabs whose movement appears to be only horizontal.

Minimize movements

- Minimize hand movements to maximize speed and smoothness.

- Many musical problems can be solved by reducing the hand movements. Keep the wrist fairly still and relaxed.

- Aim for smooth horizontal movement on the keyboard. What looks smooth, sounds smooth.

Relax

- Relax from the shoulders down to the finger tips which hold the weight of the arm and hand.

- Even fortissimo can be played with a relaxed arm but very fast attack.

What looks smooth sounds smooth.

Tips or balls of fingers

- Play on the balls of the fingers for a mellow tone, and on the tips for a brighter tone. (See *Sound Concepts: A bright or warm sound,* p53.)

Speed of attack

- A faster attack produces a louder tone;
  a slower attack produces a softer tone.

- Control the dynamics in quiet passages by adjusting the speed of
  attack, rather than holding the arm weight and tensing the shoulders.

  - If arm weight is held back in an attempt to control the
    sound, the tone will lack richness and technical control.

Balance the hand

- Balance the hand over the note(s) that are playing.

  - This minimizes jerks when moving up and down the keyboard.

  - A one-octave scale, hands separate, is a good place to
    introduce balancing the hand over the note played.

Wide leaps

Accuracy problems stemming from wide leaps can be solved by isolating
and practicing springing from one note or chord to the next like a frog
jumping from one place to another.

- This involves an up and down movement
  with the wrist but is temporary.

- The kinesthetic movement of springing trains the hand and
  when it is removed, the accuracy is almost perfect.

- This practice method is useful for literature
  as diverse as Joplin and Chopin.

Too many accents

- The remedy for too many unwanted accents is often practicing
  with accents on the downbeats and "down and up" with the
  wrist until the hands learn to coordinate. Or simply reduce
  the hand movements. (See also *Hand Coordination,* p15.)

Uneven eighth notes

- If young students play eighth notes unevenly tell them,

  - "The twin eighth notes <u>look</u> the same on the page."
    " Now make them <u>sound</u> the same in your playing."

- Check to see that they are balancing over each
  note. (See *Balance the hand,* p61.)

- Intermediate/advanced students need slow practice with
  the metronome on difficult passages with many 16th notes.
  My students do this with pulse accents on the down beat
  and gradually increase the tempo. The phrasing is added
  when the tempo is close to performance speed.

Repeated notes

- Repeated hand movement on repeated notes will
  result in repeated, unmusical accents.

- Down and up allows the wrist to go down slightly at the
  beginning of a pulse unit and then rise slowly.

  - This will also facilitate a faster speed and minimize fatigue.

  - It will also prevent the "woodpecker syndrome" which happens
    when the wrists are locked when playing repeated notes.

  - One down movement per measure is preferable to
    slow, stiff repeated notes with increasing fatigue.

Scales *(See Scales on YouTube channel: Hilda Ryan)*

Playing Scales

The unoccupied hand

- Rebalance the hand over each note allowing the rest of the
  fingers to relax. This prevents the "jerks" which happens when
  the hand must shift so fast that the attack on the first note after
  the shift is faster and louder than the surrounding notes. This
  faster attack creates an unwanted accent and unevenness.

Natural placement

- Allow the long fingers to strike the keys at the point where they fall naturally. The longer fingers will be further up in the keys and the shorter ones closer to the edge.

  - The longer fingers 2, 3 and 4 are different lengths and will naturally contact the keys at different points.

  - I like to get out eight pennies and play a B major scale slowly enough that the student can place a penny on the exact spot I have placed each finger. I then ask them to observe the position of the pennies. Almost each penny is on a different point on the keys!

The thumb and 5th finger

- Tuck the thumb immediately after playing. This preparation allows the thumb to be ready for the next time it is needed. If the thumb jerks into place, it will play with a faster attack and cause an accent.

- Play on the corner of the thumb and the tip of the 5th finger to avoid dropping the wrist and causing accents and unevenness.

Minimize movement

- Play up in the keys to avoid in and out movement on scales. Any in and out movement puts a "governor" on speed and creates unevenness.

Teaching Scales

- Introduce scales before the student encounters them in the repertoire. This way they will be in the habit of playing correctly the first time they encounter scales in the literature.

- There need be no hurry to get students to play four octave scales hands together rapidly. The primary goal is to play them correctly. Take the time to allow this to develop slowly—one octave hands separate, one octave hands together, two octaves and then four.

  - Watch scale playing closely insisting they demonstrate not only correct notes and fingering but smooth movement, balance over each note and natural placement.

    - Why? When a car driver makes an overcorrection on the road it is not too dangerous if the speed is slow. The faster the speed, however, the more magnified the overcorrection.

    - In the same way at the piano, playing a scale incorrectly at a slow tempo might not show the poor technique but at a faster tempo the unevenness will be revealed and magnified.

- All scale fingerings are the same: 1-2-3-1-2-3-4. The difference is where in the pattern the scale begins. For example, for the right hand

    - The B Major scale begins 1-2-3-1-2-3-4.

    - The E flat Major scale, on the other hand, begins in the middle of the pattern.

- Consider teaching scales in this order: B- E- A- D- G -C- F -Bb, etc.

    - The long fingers play black notes much of the time for the first scales.

    - The fingering is easier and more nearly alike on the sharp keys.

Voicing chords

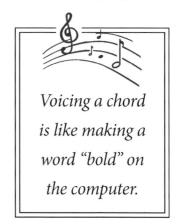

Tell the student you can't hear the top melody note clearly enough. Would they please put the top note in "bold?"

Voicing a chord is like making a word "bold" on the computer.

- Practice releasing all notes in the chord except the top melody note to program the melody clearly in the ear. In other words, there would be a legato top note and staccato notes underneath.

- If hearing it differently is not enough, then the physical aspect may help. Instruct the student to tip the hand slightly in the direction of the melody.

    - Example: If the chord is in the right hand and the melody is on top, tip the hand slightly toward the 5th finger which plays the melody.

Positioning the thumb

- Ideally, the thumb contacts the keys at the corner of the thumb.

    - If the student plays on the side of the thumb, the wrist must be lowered to do so and will cause an unwanted accent.

Speed and control

- There is of course much
  value in slow practice.

  - Early on when the metronome
    is needed, be sure the rhythmic
    grouping (often the measure)
    is maintained and the playing
    is not felt beat by beat.

- Look for extraneous up/down or in/
  out movements (technical problems)
  which may be hampering speed.
  (See *Hand movements,* p59.)

Put the intensity

in your playing,

not your

shoulders!

- Practicing a <u>shortened</u> passage <u>up to tempo</u> is often
  successful because the brain is required to focus for a very
  limited amount of time. I call this "short and fast."

- If this does not work, shorten the passage again until you find
  the amount of work the brain is ready to do at that point. As
  the days progress, the brain will be ready for longer and longer
  portions until the entire passage can be managed up to tempo.

  - What we are doing is working on developing mental
    stamina for a short period much as we must work on
    developing the ability to focus deeply for longer and longer
    periods of time when preparing a full-length recital.

  - The real problem is not that the fingers cannot
    play fast, but that the fingers can play faster than
    the brain can process. The brain needs to develop
    mental stamina and this is best accomplished by
    practicing little bits fast, gradually linking the bits
    together as the brain develops mental endurance.

  - This is particularly useful in the finishing stages
    when the performance tempo seems out of reach.
    Working with the metronome is quite often the
    best choice early in the learning process.

▶ **Short technical videos on YouTube channel: Hilda Ryan**

- Scales

- Octaves

- Broken octaves

- Arpeggios

- 7-minute technical warm-up

TEMPO

Crescendo problems

- Students have a tendency to play faster during a crescendo.
- Encourage them to put the intensity in the dynamics instead.

Determining the tempo

- Tempo is determined in part by the harmonic speed.
- Pieces with fast moving harmonies need to be kept to a slower tempo to allow the listener to assimilate the harmonic movement.
  - The Chopin Prelude in C Minor has harmonies that change with every quarter note, necessitating a slower tempo.
  - The Chopin Prelude in B Minor has the same chord for entire measures and needs to move along.

Optimum practice tempo

- Slow enough to be 95% accurate
- Fast enough to be in pulse
- Speed should come on top of ease

Speed should come on top of ease.

Tempo fluctuation

- If there is a problem with tempo fluctuation, try using the metronome. If it is a longer piece, sample each section by playing a few bars of each passage with a different pattern to program a consistent tempo in the ear.

- Put the metronome on silent mode while playing through the piece, glancing over several times.

THEORY

Understanding the theory and harmonic structure of a piece unlocks its secrets and paves the way for an organic interpretation based on the theory.

Lesson time is well spent understanding the form, chordal structure, etc. Theory is much more than an exam or competition preparation. Discover together with your student what is there and lead them to discover <u>why</u> the composer wrote a crescendo or a ritard. This fosters musical independence.

If a student understands why the crescendo or ritard is there, then <u>they</u> will feel the need to get louder or slower for a musical reason, not just because it is written in the music or the teachers says to do so. The playing is far more convincing from a listener or judge's standpoint, and appreciably more satisfying to the student performer as well.

Many times during a lesson I have an insight into the composer's intent and share it with the student. It delights both the student and me! Teaching music by the masters is such a privilege and I want my students to know why they are master composers.

Diminished seventh chords

- Because all the intervals in a fully diminished 7th chords are the same, there is no aural "root" to the chord, no sense of repose or "home." Composers love to use these chords for passages with increasing intensity. Point this out to the intermediate/advanced student.

- A diminished 7th chord is like an inch worm who appears to have no head or tail!

> A diminished 7th chord is like an inch worm!
> No head, no tail!

Minor scales

- Students often confuse relative and parallel minor.
  Here is one way to explain it.

  - The <u>relative</u> minor has the same key signature but starts
    on a different note. It is like a family cousin, with the same
    last name, who probably lives in a different city.

  - The <u>parallel</u> minor has the same starting note but a
    different key signature and is like a family friend who
    lives in the same city but has a different last name.

- Students will need a review of minor scales several times after
  encountering them in a theory book. Use the lesson pieces as a
  built-in form of a reminder. Ask the student, "What is the key?"

  - Landmarks and key signatures, likewise, need review many times.
    Online music theory games can be very helpful.
    (See Theory on the Web at www.hildaryan.com.)

Modulations

- The simplest way to modulate is to find the
  way to the dominant of the new key.

- The dominant of the new key is like the door of a house. When
  you open the door, you are in the house. When you arrive at
  the dominant, you are ready to take off in the new key.

  > **The dominant of the new key
  > is like the door to a house.**

Triads and inversions

- When <u>explaining inversions</u> for the first time I often use this illustration:

  - Inverting a triad is like playing leapfrog with three people.
    The person at the back leaps over the other two. The same
    three people "invert" their order much as the bottom note
    in a triad "jumps" over the other two and lands on top.

> **Finding the notes for a triad and its inversions is like playing leapfrog.**

- When a student <u>continues to make note mistakes</u> when playing inversions I often use this illustration:

  - If we decide to take a picture of you (student) and your brother and sister, we might start with you in the middle. Then we might change the order and put your sister in the middle, etc. but the picture always has the same three people in it—you, your brother and sister. In music, each inversion has the same three notes, so if the chords sound wrong, check to make sure you have the same three notes.

    > **Playing triads and inversions is like taking a picture.**

OTHER BOOKS BY HILDA RYAN AVAILABLE ON AMAZON.COM AND TOP MUSIC MARKETPLACE

Instant Organization for Your Piano Studio, 25+ Reproducible Forms

Forms for all aspects of piano teaching are included with rights to reproduce year after year. Create a Teacher Notebook that helps you keep up with recital plans, tuition payments, tax records, etc. as well as sections for each student with new student information, semester plan sheets and evaluations. Business forms for billing and purchasing music are also included as well as sample studio guidelines, enrollment agreement and a number of studio ideas. Ebook includes a choice of Teacher Notebook covers to print as well.

Teaching Articulation: Classical Collection for Piano

Easiest original piano pieces by master composers are presented in a pedagogical sequence that teaches contrasting articulation. The book begins at a reading level of simple counterpoint, and the student is led step by step from parallel articulation to contrasting articulation. Along the way students are given practical tips on pulse, balance and shaping phrases. Each new section of the book is preceded by tips "To the Student" and "To the Teacher," a special feature providing guidance on the concepts.

This volume bridges the gap between the early method books and the style collections. Students completing this book will be ready to encounter the contrasting articulation challenges presented in the many wonderful collections on the market.

Folk Tunes in All the Keys with Harmonization, Transposition & Improvisation

Folk Tunes in All the Keys with Harmonization, Transposition & Improvisation provides a delightful way to address proficiency skills within its 45 beautiful folk melodies from around the world. Students are asked to play and transpose two folk tunes and harmonize two more folk tunes in all the major keys. Melodies are single note and accompaniments are variations of the simple block chord cadence using only I, IV & V chords. At the end of the book 50 one-measure improvisation patterns are given and the student is encouraged to play through the pieces again using one or more of the patterns.

VIDEOS BY HILDA RYAN

Videos on Teaching Topics — *New videos are posted every Friday.*

Practical 1 topic / 2-minute videos incorporating the Quick Tips concepts:

- Subscribe to YouTube channel: Hilda Ryan
- Like me on Facebook at: Quick Tips for Piano Teachers
- Follow me on Instagram at: QuickTips4PianoTeachers

Videos on Scales • Octaves • Broken Octaves • Arpeggios

For short technical videos see earliest posted videos on
YouTube channel: Hilda Ryan.

RECOMMENDED BOOKS

The following books would be helpful for
a more in-depth look at the concepts in this book.

Camp, Max W. *Teaching Piano: The Synthesis of Mind, Ear and Body.*
Los Angeles: Alfred Music, 1992.

Lhevinne, Josef. *Basic Principles in Pianoforte Playing.*
New York: Dover Publications, Revised edition 1972.

Lloyd-Watts, Valery/Carole L. Bigler. *Ornamentation, A Question and Answer Manual.* Van Nuys: Alfred Publishing, 1995.

Whiteside, Abby. *Indispensables of Piano Playing.*
New York: Scribner's, 1961.

Made in United States
Orlando, FL
27 May 2022

18238723R00048